ALSO BY SANDRA AND DANIEL BISKIND

The CODEBREAKER PLATINUM Series

PEACE: Power Up Your Life

LOVE
IGNITE THE SECRET TO YOUR SUCCESS

SANDRA AND DANIEL BISKIND

Second in The CODEBREAKER PLATINUM Series

LOVE: Ignite The Secret To Your Success
Second in The CODEBREAKER PLATINUM Series
Version 1.1

Copyright © 2015 Sandra and Daniel Biskind

ALL RIGHTS RESERVED. This book contains material protected under International and Federal Copyright Laws and Treaties. Any unauthorized reprint or use of this material is prohibited. No part of this book may be reproduced or transmitted in any form or by any means, electronic or mechanical, including photocopying, recording, or by any information storage and retrieval system without express written permission from the author/publisher.

Because of the dynamic nature of the Internet, any web addresses or links contained in this book may have changed since publication and may no longer be valid.

The purpose of this book is to educate and inspire. The authors and/or publisher do not guarantee that anyone following these techniques, suggestions, tools, ideas or strategies will have the same results that other people have attained. The author and/or publisher shall have neither liability nor responsibility to anyone with respect to any loss or damage caused, or alleged to be caused, directly or indirectly.

The authors of this book do not dispense medical advice or prescribe the use of any technique or tool as a form of treatment for physical, emotional, or medical problems without the advice of a physician, either directly or indirectly. The intent of the authors is to offer information of a general and educational nature to help you in your quest for emotional and spiritual well-being. In the event you use any of the information in this book or from our websites or workshops, which is your constitutional right, the authors and the publisher assume no responsibility for your actions.

Published by EMISSARY COMMUNICATIONS LLC

CAUTION: SPIRITUALLY INTOXICATING!

Do not drive or operate heavy machinery while under the influence of this book.

ACCLAIM FOR SANDRA AND DANIEL BISKIND

JACK CANFIELD - Co-author of *Chicken Soup for the Soul* series, *The Success Principles* and a featured teacher in the film, *The Secret*

Sandra and Daniel are profound healers, trainers, speakers and authors who do some exceptional transformational work. I've experienced their work and found it truly life changing — so much so that I had them work with my entire staff with magical results. They have an amazing ability to shift energy and remove blocks on very deep levels.

From the first time I sat down with them I knew something special and profound was about to happen. Their unconditional love, joy and radiance fills the room. An hour later I left more calm, more centered, more my true self and more creative than I can remember. They are the real deal and I highly recommend them and their work. It is transformational wizardry at its best.

WILLIAM BRYANT - Former Chairman of the Board, American Chamber of Commerce Executives

Thank you beyond words for conceiving and writing *"PEACE: Power Up Your Life,"* the first book in your CODEBREAKER PLATINUM Series.

Some years ago I was the President and CEO of the largest metropolitan Chamber of Commerce in the United States. If I would have had this publication at that time, our transformation work would have been more efficient, and for sure, more peaceful. Count on this: the first thing I would have done would have been to furnish copies of *"PEACE"* to my Board of Directors, our entire staff and to all my family members. Simply fantastic! If the next book in your series is just half as enlightening, I may just un-retire.

DEREK RYDAL - Transformational coach, best-selling author, creator of The Law of Emergence

"I've worked with a lot of healers, but rarely do I meet one who is as quick to the heart of the matter as Sandra. In a matter of minutes, she was tuned into the core issues I was dealing with and the root causes, and a few minutes later I could feel a tangible shift, like a weight had been lifted and a new level of energy had been opened. Something was palpably different about me — and all of this in minutes - not months! I look forward to what's possible with her incredible work, and encourage anyone struggling with issues (especially the seemingly unsolvable ones) to experience this for themselves."

GARY RUSH - Anthony Robbins Business and Success Coach,

For all my life I have been uncomfortable expressing love to the people closest to me. There has always been this resistance to express the one emotion that is the essence of our existence.

As a result, there has always been this hole in my life that I ignored and that has denied me the depth and richness of life I deserve. Sandra, in just three sessions, nailed what had happened in my past and knew what was preventing me from being the person I so desperately wanted to be. She has a rare gift and talent to pick up what the blocks are and how to resolve them. As a coach for Tony Robbins and with many mentors in personal development, I know for a fact that very few have this ability.

After working with her I feel more at peace with myself and know that I am now on track to express and experience more love in my life.

ALISON HORA - Professional Dive Instructor

To sift through my thoughts and find a completely different person than two days ago has brought me to a place of great appreciation and Sandra I need to thank you for this. For me the amazement of your work, is that my life's structure is still there, people didn't disappear. But, my deep emotions have changed. The shift that has taken place within me is unbelievable.

If I was asked two days ago if it were possible to be clear and free from such deep inner pain and confusion so quickly, my answer would have been no. I would not have been able to even imagine my way to this place that I am now at. In the mornings I now wake with excitement for my life. My energy levels have been restored and I am happy and so truly honored to have met you.

AMBER BRECH-HOLLINS - Special Events Photographer

One of the most important decisions I have ever made in my life was to work on a personal level with Sandra and Daniel. I have worked with them for more than 8 years because doing this work shifts me from crisis point to a place of absolute relief and neutrality in a matter of minutes.

It has transformed my life on every level and in every part of my life dramatically and continues to do so. Whether it be for me personally with something I'm working on or in my relationships with my husband, children, work colleagues, family & friends or in my businesses, every area is enriched and improved.

I am forever grateful for the peace and joy that it brings me back to. For bringing me back to my true self. My true north. Thank you, Sandra and Daniel.

ROBERT HURST - Business Owner and Entrepreneur

To say I am passionate about the new and improved direction in my life would be an understatement. I feel like an i7 processor in a 386 world. I have used Jim Rohn, Tony Robbins, Dennis Waitley and many others over the last 30 years. Nothing I have ever done can compare to the breakthrough technology that I have been lucky enough to experience through Sandra and Daniel and their Ultimate Mind Shift program.

JAMES HOLLINS - Business Owner and Entrepreneur

WOW! Words almost can't do justice to the incredible work that Sandra and Daniel do. To be able to go from totally on edge, stressed, depressed, angry, and "over life", to feeling happy, content, aligned, powerful, strong, and "in love" with life again, all in the space of a thirty minute session — Truly amazing! I really appreciate being ME again.

ALISON QUEDLEY - Former publisher and editor IN TOUCH magazine

The books in The CODEBREAKER PLATINUM Series are AMAZING just like you both. It comes straight from the heart and is written so deceptively simply. I am sure that people reading it will absorb the words on a very deep level without even realising the changes the words will be making in their lives!! This is a life changing book for anyone who is in any pain and distress, as well as those who want to carry on their journey into the Divine Mind and Love.

Can't wait until I can hold *CODEBREAKER: Discover the Password to Unlock The Best Version Of You* in my hands and feel the power of healing that I know will affect many many souls.

Thank you both for your dedication to humanity and for your ever present loving connection.

CONTENTS

Introduction: The Codebreaker Platinum Series 11
A Brief Explanation Of Terms 14
How To Use The Codebreaker Platinum Series 17
Map Of Awareness 19
The Master Password 22
What Is Enlightenment? 27
What Is Love? 31
I Know The Way You Can Get 32
You Are What You Are Looking For 34
Love In The Shower 36
After The Loss 39
The Hole In The Heart Can Be Made To Disappear 41
Love: The Underestimated Genius Of The Heart 45
Love At One Hundred And Six 47
Open Sesame 50
Painful Games 51
The Science Of Love 54
Transcendent Vibrations 57
Past, Present, And Future Programs 59
Alternative Lives? 60
The Happiness Factor 64
The Need For Loving Family Connections 67

An Ancient Parable For Today 70
Neurons Firing On All Cylinders 72
The Codebreaker Success Frequency 75
True Self Reprogramming 79
A Meditation On Love:
    Ignite The Secret To Your Success 82
Ego Puppy Training #2: Love 85
Jumpstart The Process 89
The Four Questions: Love 91
Rate Your State: Love 93
The Ultimate Mind Shift: An Introduction
    To Quantum Neutrality—The First Steps 96
A Quick Overview: Love 100
About Sandra And Daniel 108
From Sandra And Daniel 110
Appreciation 112
Become The Best Version of You 115

INTRODUCTION
The CODEBREAKER PLATINUM Series

"When you are connected to your Divine Mind, you will feel an ocean of peace and joy moving in you."

—Sandra and Daniel Biskind

The only thing you can be 100% certain of in your future is being yourself. Which version are you going to be?

This book and all the books, programs, and website materials in The CODEBREAKER PLATINUM Series have been conceived and designed to empower you to become the best version of you. Now, more than at any other time in history, there is the emerging potential to make huge shifts in consciousness that can take humanity—and yes, individuals—into a whole new stratosphere of living with peace and love, expanded awareness, confidence, and trust; integrity and empowered neutrality; and mindful oneness with one another and the cosmos.

Collectively, the evolution of our souls is accelerating the realization of the new human: awakened, enlightened, self-actualized and whole. Welcome! This book is dedicated to accelerating your transformation—to supporting your rapid change and profound inner growth.

We are all searching for the same thing. We all want peace, love and joy. We all want to be happy.

An attractive, sixty-year-old American woman, who had never been married and who lived alone with her cat, decided to attend one of our weekend seminars in Los Angeles. She was ever hopeful of finding resolution around an ongoing, emotionally debilitating problem. She was extremely successful in her career and had become a woman of means who had spent 40 years and hundreds of thousands of dollars trying to find peace around an incestuous experience in her teens that continued to torment her and sabotage her life. During a private session after the weekend, we were able to discover the core program that was blocking her from being able to step into her true personal power.

Her emotions around the event were rendered neutral, which enabled her to finally release the negative life pattern ruining her life. In just one session, she shifted from someone who was still traumatized and afraid of never having a fulfilling and meaningful relationship to finally feeling peaceful and optimistic about her future. She was happy.

Happiness often eludes us. Most people are in denial of this truth, which is exactly the way the ego mind likes it. Your ego mind has you seeking pleasure in all the wrong places to alleviate the pain of loneliness and sadness and to distract you from feelings of emptiness and lack of meaning and fulfillment.

Daniel and I both had to overcome many debilitating life challenges where we had to find the inner strength and personal power to thrive in adversity. It was this work that helped us through the tough times and brought us back into alignment with our True Selves. We kept course correcting back into our hearts until peace and love were restored.

To experience the richness of life, of real love and authentic forgiveness, we first had to master our minds in order to come to that place of peace and love. We needed to have gratitude for all we had and all we could give.

Having reached that place inside ourselves and having assisted thousands of people around the world to do likewise, we knew the next step in living our life purpose was to write these books. We want to share with you the tools and gifts we have developed over our lifetimes to transform our lives so that you can do the same.

More than encouragement, the books in The CODEBREAKER PLATINUM Series act as guides and mentors on your amazing journey from the head to the heart. For some, this series will provide stimulating new ideas. For others, it will provide confirmation that you are on the right track to everyday enlightenment.

You don't have to change your religious or spiritual beliefs for these books to weave miracles in your life. Remember, you are not alone. To varying degrees, we all face the same challenges. And depending on the software programs you are running in your unique human computer, you will create different levels of emotional adjustment as you deal with those challenges.

No matter how daunting or overwhelming your circumstances may seem, just like Daniel and me (along with many others), you can turn your life around.

As you read, absorb, and apply The CODEBREAKER PLATINUM Master Password, you will begin to retrain your mind and transform your emotions and your experience of life. Reconnecting with the love that you are will accelerate your soul's evolution into enlightenment and wholeness. This will in turn propel you into greater levels of inner peace, joy, happiness, and optimal health- and a closer connection to the divine within you.

A BRIEF EXPLANATION OF TERMS

Some concepts basic to our work include your True Self, Ego mind programs, Neutrality, The Divine Mind, Living a PLATINUM life and Non-duality.

YOUR TRUE SELF is the perfection of who you really are, and love is an eternal expression of your True Self, which is whole and complete.

EGO MIND PROGRAMS are parts of your self image that you've fabricated as opposed to the perfection of your True Self. Say you have an ego mind program that you believe you are not worthy of love. You will then create situations that prove that. You can't help but sabotage your career, your relationships, and your health when you believe you can never experience love.

NEUTRALITY is a state in which you are free of belief and attachment. Neutrality's open-mindedness enables you to access higher awareness, free of bias, emotion and prejudice. The state of empowered Neutrality is where your ego mind's thoughts and emotions no longer control you. Neutrality is essential to love, peace and real freedom and is the key to enlightenment.

THE DIVINE MIND is the ever-expanding, infinite expression of pure love and joy that expresses itself deep within you when you are no longer held hostage by the ego mind but are free and at peace. It is the source of true reality in contrast to ego mind which is the source of false reality.

LIVING A PLATINUM LIFE means you have the skills to remain neutral and empowered regardless of circumstances. A PLATINUM life enables you to live the perfection that you really are free of limiting beliefs and ideas—free of inner turmoil.

Your relationships become more stable; you feel happier and healthier; more vital and creative. With less useless mind chatter, you have a more balanced emotional life. You are in touch with the field of infinite possibilities.

In a PLATINUM life you are continually becoming the best version of you.

NON-DUALITY is the natural foundational state of awareness of the unity of subject and object. It is where we understand we are all connected, not only to each other but to our Source and to all life.

> **"We need to understand that thoughts are tools. Are we using them as productively as we can? Are our thoughts serving us well, or are we their victims? It's up to us."**
>
> *—Dr. Tom Morris*

HOW TO USE
The CODEBREAKER PLATINUM Series

THE WORK: No matter where you are on your own mystical journey into the real world of infinite love, peace, joy and true success you can use these tools and techniques to begin or continue to realign yourself with the high frequencies of the Divine Mind Code.

FIRST AID: Use *LOVE: Ignite The Secret To Your Success* as a mentor when you need help on any level. Focus your intention on receiving the guidance you need, open the book randomly, and the chapter or page you see will be what you need to read in that moment. Or, if you prefer, look at the contents page and then read the appropriate section to help you instantly feel better.

THE DIVINE MIND FIELD: Use this book as a way to attune yourself to the frequency of the Divine Mind Code—accessible through your wholistic consciousness, which incorporates the maximal range of the human mind. The CODEBREAKER PLATINUM books activate the Master Password so your True Self's attributes of peace, love, awareness, trust, integrity, neutrality, unity and mindfulness are experienced—reconnecting you to your personal power.

POEMS: When a poem appears, take a deep breath and relax. Do not rush through it, but savor it. Each one has been deliberately chosen to catapult you into your heart and illuminate your soul, flicking the switch on the light within. Join these high frequency beings as they bare their God-drenched souls as often as you can.

MEDITATIONS AND VISUALIZATIONS: Simple meditations will attune you to the frequency of the relevant quality in each chapter. Repeating them will also help create new neural pathways in the brain. Eventually these pathways become the dominant thought processing pathways that help raise your level of awareness. Download your free CODEBREAKER PLATINUM meditations at www.TheBiskinds.com.

THE TOOL KIT: Simple three point "keys" give you a fast and easy way to receive and assimilate information. Read and contemplate them REPEATEDLY until they become like short passwords themselves. They will simply and effectively unlock your life code to access your personal power.

REPROGRAMMING THE BRAIN: Training the brain via repetition is also an essential way for you to learn. As you create new habit fields in the mind, they become reflected as new neural pathways that change the way the brain functions.

The teachings will be repeated in short stories, metaphors and analogies going over the same points in different contexts. Override your ego mind's voice when it tells you, "I have heard it all before."

As one of my teachers in Australia said, "Because I love you so much, I will continue to give you the same information until you are living it."

To maximize its transformational effect in your life, it is important to not only read this book often but to immerse yourself in it—using the practices daily.

MAP OF AWARENESS

Daniel and I have long been considered experts in the art and science of personal transformation. We have helped thousands of people around the world, from London and New York to Los Angeles and Australasia. In our ongoing research and development, we discovered the Master Password that unlocks the Divine Mind Code for us. It was a fascinating process that revealed a code of such depth that we missed its power at first.

We took our time, as we are asking you to do. As you begin to work with this secret password, multiple uses will be revealed for each concept. People who have read these books three and four times have said that it became even more useful, insightful, and life-changing the more they read them.

We created a Map of Awareness inspired by the Hawkins scale of consciousness from the book *Power vs. Force: The Hidden Determinants of Human Behavior* by David Hawkins, M.D., Ph.D.

The Hawkins scale is a two-dimensional, measuring consciousness in a vertical line going from 0 to 1,000 with 0 being the lowest state of consciousness. The majority of people are either 200 or below and are firmly entrenched in ego mind thinking. No one at this level of consciousness would even consider picking up, let alone reading, *LOVE: Ignite The Secret To Your Success* or *The CODEBREAKER PLATINUM Series*.

Hawkins calibrated Einstein's consciousness at 499, which he considered the pinnacle of intellect. At 500, your heart opens and you begin to operate out of love. The state of unconditional love begins at 540. Enlightened states calibrate from 600 to 1,000, the theoretical maximum sustainable in a human body. Humanity's greatest masters, including Buddha and Jesus, calibrated at 1,000.

The Integrated Wholeness Scale is three dimensional and logarithmic. It adds a horizontal axis that measures personality issues that need to be resolved as you move from one level of awareness to another. Life challenges can trigger negative emotional responses and all the associated issues. As you move farther along both consciousness and personality sides of the scale together, the way you deal with them becomes more efficient and effective.

Unpacking personality programs from consciousness helps us to understand how high-consciousness people can do otherwise inexplicably low-consciousness deeds.

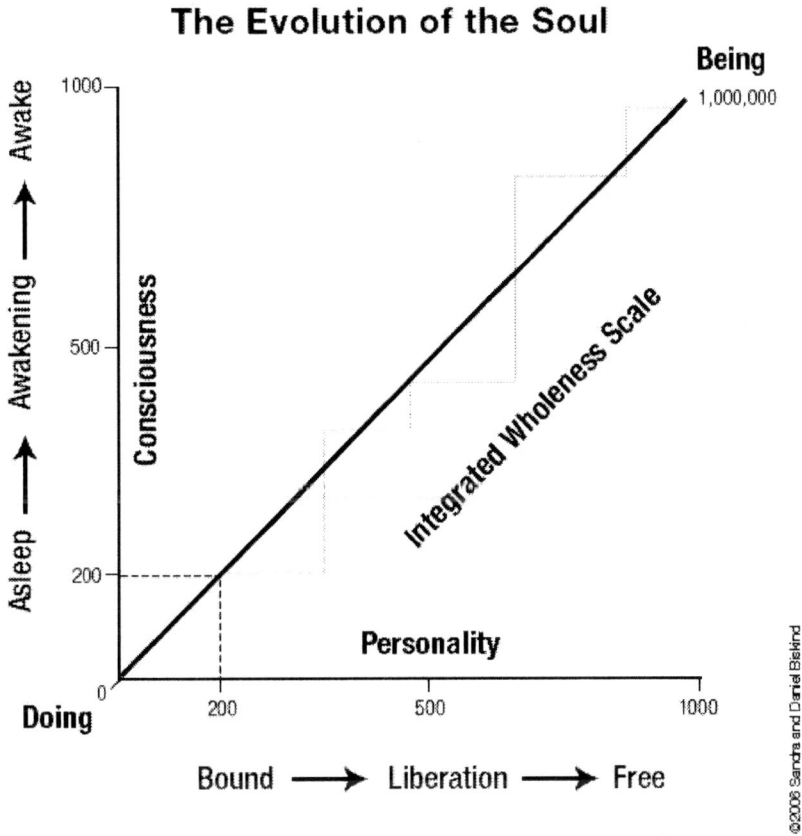

The CODEBREAKER PLATINUM Series presents a life-long process of revelation, mastery, and ongoing practice and training. The immense power and beauty of your True Self is revealed increasingly with every book in the series. The words you are about to read will take you into a place where the mystical world of the Divine Mind guides your life and you are no longer held hostage in the fantasy world of your ego mind. Join us on this inner exploration of the non-dual world that is your True Self.

THE MASTER PASSWORD

Here is The CODEBREAKER Master Password:

PEACE LOVE AWARENESS TRUST
INTEGRITY NEUTRALITY UNITY MINDFULNESS

PLATINUM is the Master Password that in the correct combination unlocks the secret to the Divine Mind Code for each us.

This Master Password is like a key that awakens your consciousness and liberates your personality. As Buddha said, "Your mind is everything. What you think you become." You can train your mind, be accountable for your soul choices, attune yourself to the Divine Mind Code and ascend the Integrated Wholeness Scale into enlightened states.

PLATINUM unlocks the code to the inspiring, uplifting, true stories of the heart rather than perpetuating the deceptive, destructive, fictitious stories of the ego mind. This series presents a plan which makes your soul's choice to live by the wisdom of the Divine Mind Code rather than the dictates of the ego mind code a whole lot easier.

You can easily discover the passwords to your ego mind codes, and in doing so reveal the truth that you have been compromised and corrupted by the enemy within—the ego mind.

Some of them go something like this: pathetic, loser, asshole, terrorist, intolerant, negative, unforgivable, malicious.

These words are below 100 on both the consciousness axis and personality axis of the Integrated Wholeness Scale.

PLATINUM acknowledges you are already perfect and you are much more than the mere sum of your automated programs, conditioned thinking and mindless self-talk. And, as you so well know, you are much more than what your physical senses reveal.

You are a PLATINUM being. This is your True Self. Most people never realize this because their soul is asleep. They sleepwalk through life. Activating the PLATINUM password awakens your soul to choose wholeness again.

Learn to use the password to decode your life and break through to great loving relationships, real strength and vitality, and the work and financial success you deserve.

Make the commitment to start living your PLATINUM life today.

As you read, absorb, and implement these concepts you will retrain your mind, which transforms your experience of life. Accelerate your soul's journey into enlightenment and wholeness and propel yourself into greater levels of love, joy, inner peace, happiness, better health, and a closer connection to the divine perfection within you.

Uh oh! What do I have to give up to live a PLATINUM life?

Sex, wine, shopping, credit cards…just kidding! Seriously, you will only be giving up your illusions and stories. You won't miss any of the things you have to give up to live a PLATINUM life, but you will naturally feel better and your light will shine brighter and you will attract more love in your life. And, you will have loads of fun.

You have no doubt already learned that you can think positively about what you desire until you are blue in the face, but that does not mean those positive thoughts will manifest as changes in your life. Ultimately, your unconscious programs and patterns are running the show. Until those are corrected your ability to manifest your best intentions will continue to be sabotaged by programs hidden in your unconscious mind.

Your life is a masterpiece in the making. Let us help you fulfill your purpose by changing the inner landscape of your life so the outer landscape of your home, your work, and your relationships can reflect the change you want to be and see.

> *"When love and skill work together,*
> *expect a masterpiece."*
>
> —John Ruskin

The CODEBREAKER PLATINUM Series presents groundbreaking concepts that will empower you to move into new levels of peace, love, and awareness, which lead to whole new ways of being. The aim of this system is for you to have a complete mind shift. That is why we call the process The Ultimate Mind Shift™.

This series has been intentionally designed to attune you to the supercharged frequency of enlightenment. You could feel very high and sometimes the brain may feel heavy because the energy field created as you read these books reconnects you to the enlightenment frequency. Its vibrational field, including the superconscious frequency of higher awareness, extends beyond that of the conscious and unconscious minds. As your brain processes them, you may experience new and different sensations.

Use The CODEBREAKER PLATINUM password to crack the Divine Mind Code and start living the life of your dreams. As you read through these books, and as you pick up and implement the Key Passwords one at a time, and then put them together, you will create your own version of the extravagantly rich and beautiful life presented to you in this process of enlightenment.

To maximize the transformational impact in your life, it is important to not only read these books often but to immerse yourself in them and to use the tools on a daily basis.

Here is what you will get out of reading *LOVE: Ignite The Secret To Your Success* and from using the Ultimate Mind Shift™ teaching and training process:

- Increase your emotional intelligence, identify problematic habitual emotional responses to conflict in your life, and implement a powerful new strategy to resolve them while keeping peace of mind.
- Develop a strong, unwavering relationship with your True Self and an ability to understand and utilize your inner communication when making decisions in your everyday life.
- Receive energy that supports you and helps you love, and feel loved and understood, regardless of conditions in your external world.
- Create new patterns and habits that support your health and well-being.
- Create the deep and lasting relationship of your dreams with your partner or future partner.
- Experience deeper love and connection and better communication with the people in your life.
- Become more energetically attractive and magnetic.
- Discover deeper meaning and purpose in your life.

- Delete old sabotage programs to free you to be more creative.
- Access your real power and strength, and lead through love.
- Silence the chatter of your ego mind, and master your inner critic.
- Strengthen your connection to your spiritual core to live in a calm and balanced place no matter what life throws at you.
- Experience an energetic frequency that regenerates, rejuvenates, strengthens, and renews every cell in your body.
- Access the mystical world of the Divine Mind which automatically brings your body, mind, and soul into higher levels of awareness.
- Mastery of the simple tools that progressively build a deeper and more sustainable connection to the PLATINUM password and the Divine Mind Code.
- A level of happiness that will astonish and delight you.

Have fun! And remember,

The secret to enlightenment is to lighten up!

WHAT IS ENLIGHTENMENT?

Enlightenment is the state in which you are fully connected to your True Self, often characterized by causeless love and limitless joy.

It is the state where you experience the world without projecting judgment.

Enlightenment empowers you to accept the perfection in everyone and love them without reservation or condition.

It is the peaceful, confident experience of life unfiltered by the programs of your ego mind. In enlightenment, the world is simply a mirror of you and the divine energy within you.

> *"It isn't by getting out of the world that we become enlightened, but by getting into the world...by getting so tuned in that we can ride the waves of our existence and never get tossed because we become the waves."*
>
> *–Ken Kesey*

Like many people, have you ever thought, "I don't want to be enlightened and live alone high on a mountain top, laughing at the rest of the world?" After a lifetime's desire to know, understand and live an enlightened life, both Daniel and I have discovered that is not what enlightenment is about at all.

I was fortunate to have spent many years working with an enlightened American spiritual teacher who visited

Melbourne a few times a year. I had just taken a seat when I realized the whole auditorium was full of an intense, iridescent purple light. But where was it coming from? I had been putting on stage shows for many years and had used lighting technicians for special effects many times. No matter where I looked I could not find the banks of lights that would have been needed to fill the whole room with this gorgeous wash of colored light.

I asked the person sitting beside me if they knew why our teacher was using purple light and could he see where the light was coming from. He looked at me quizzically and said in an are-you-for-real voice, "What purple light? There's no purple light on the stage, or in the room." Well, there was purple light in the room I was sitting in! In exasperation, I closed my eyes. The same purple light was flooding my internal world.

So that's where it was coming from—inside me! I was the source of light. When asked, the teacher told me the purple light I was seeing was my own spirit. Obviously I could see this light with my physical eyes but who was seeing it when my eyes were closed? It was my soul—the observer—that part of me that can never die and is capable of fully connecting to my True Self. Like my physical eyes, my spiritual eyes were observing and relaying messages to the brain to process.

I had been working with this spiritual master for over six years and in that time had changed the way I lived my life. I was meditating on a daily basis and still working with other amazing healers and teachers to hone my own ability to be the best version of myself.

I realized that I coped with life challenges with more ease and less drama and was capable of being even more creative, more loving, and more forgiving than ever. And, I was totally addicted to the high of enlightenment. Feelings of joy and love would overwhelm me for no reason at all. I would see total strangers and be in love with all of them—no matter what they looked like. If this was an enlightened state, I wanted more.

During a public session with an Indian guru who was visiting Melbourne, a few hundred people were all invited to come to the front of the room for a hug with this enlightened being. I waited in line for over half an hour. (I would have waited even if I was the last person in line and it was a very long line.) When she held me in her arms close to her chest, she just said, "More. More. More." That became my mantra. More love, more joy, more wonder and fulfilment. If this was an enlightenment state and being connected to my Divine Mind I was on the right path.

In the enlightened state, you understand the great mysteries of life, including that the whole of humanity is one wonderful idea from the mind of God which is manifesting in 7 billion unique ways. From an enlightened perspective, you understand humanity has been hoodwinked into believing what the ego mind has told us—that we are separate from everyone else and need to look outside ourselves for the love, joy, success, health, and well-being that we seek.

"Enlightenment is your natural state and your thoughts are the only thing stopping you from having the life you want."

—Sandra Biskind

WHAT IS LOVE?

*Pure love is your essence.
Your purpose is to grow, evolve, and have
fun expressing the love that you are.*

Love is a state and an energy, not an emotion. As energy, it is the most powerful energy of the cosmos. It is the catalyst of creation and creativity and is infinitely powerful.

Love is the fuel of miracles.

At your very core, Love is who you are. Love is an expression of your perfection when unimpeded by ego mind programs.

As your True Self, love is inextricably interwoven with enlightenment, forgiveness, peace, and success on every level of existence.

Without love it is impossible to successfully live a PLATINUM life because more than anything else, love facilitates transformation.

Your Divine Mind Code is founded on love. It is filled with authenticity, openness, transparency, acceptance, empathy and respect. It supports the development and growth of real success and happiness.

When you have not yet awakened to the love that is your True Self, it is easy for the ego mind to fool you into believing true love is somewhere "out there." No wonder every person at some stage has been looking for love in all the wrong places.

I KNOW THE WAY YOU CAN GET

I know the way you can get
When you have not had a drink of Love:

Your face hardens,
Your sweet muscles cramp.
Children become concerned
About a strange look that appears in your eyes
Which even begins to worry your own mirror
And nose.

Squirrels and birds sense your sadness
And call an important conference in a tall tree.
They decide which secret code to chant
To help your mind and soul.

Even angels fear that brand of madness
That arrays itself against the world
And throws sharp stones and spears into
The innocent
And into one's self.

O I know the way you can get
If you have not been drinking Love:

You might rip apart
Every sentence your friends and teachers say,
Looking for hidden clauses.

You might weigh every word on a scale
Like a dead fish.

You might pull out a ruler to measure
From every angle in your darkness
The beautiful dimensions of a heart you once
Trusted.

I know the way you can get
If you have not had a drink from Love's
Hands.

That is why all the Great Ones speak of
The vital need
To keep remembering God,
So you will come to know and see Him
As being so Playful
And Wanting,
Just Wanting to help.

That is why Hafiz says:
Bring your cup near me.
For all I care about
Is quenching your thirst for freedom!

All a Sane man can ever care about
Is giving Love!

–Hafiz (translated by Daniel Ladinsky)

From the Penguin publication *I Heard God Laughing: Poems of Hope and Joy.* Copyright 1996 & 2006 by Daniel Ladinsky and used with his permission.

YOU ARE WHAT YOU ARE LOOKING FOR

"When the power of Love overcomes the love of power, the world will know peace."

—Jimi Hendrix

In virtually every spiritual and religious tradition there is an archetypal story or myth about what is often called "the pearl of great price." Let's imagine it is time for God to give you the most precious gift of all—to give you the pearl of great price.

It is the gift of unconditional love. In truth, it is the love that you are.

In this story, God knows you will place greater value on this gift if you think it is precious and something to be treasured. He wanted to hide this gift in the last place you would look to ensure that when you finally found it, you would value it and not throw it back from whence it came.

As God pondered this, He had the idea to hide it in the ocean at the bottom of the deepest abyss. Oh no, that would not work; the Russians would go there and find it. Then He thought to place this gift on top of the highest mountain peak. But that would not work either; the English would go there. Hmmm, what if it was placed on the moon? No, that still wouldn't work; the Americans will go there.

At last God realized He could place this invaluable gift in the one place you would never think to look—right in the center of your heart.

You are looking into your heart now and are surprised to find that all the cosmos and more lives there with you. It is the longest expedition you and all of humanity will have ever undertaken on this journey from the head into the heart—and the most rewarding.

> *"And still, after all this time, the sun*
> *has never said to the earth,*
> *you owe me.*
> *Look what happens*
> *with love like that.*
> *It lights up the sky."*
>
> —*Rumi*

Daniel and I have long lived by Divine Guidance, so it is hardly surprising that just after dinner on our second date, the two of us agreed we were married as of that moment. Obviously, there was something very powerful going on for two people who had only met moments before to be that certain of such a huge commitment.

We had spent our lives diligently exploring the human potential movement and pursuing the mystical in the same headlong fashion we had pursued our business goals: tuned into our Divine guidance, 100% commitment and full speed ahead. We both had many indescribable experiences outside the understanding of the ego mind and institutional science. Fortunately, mainstream scientists are now moving closer to the wisdom of the formerly inexplicable spiritual world that Eastern mystics have known for thousands of years.

Our relationship triggered off so many "other worldly" events that it would take a whole book to tell them, but as we are in *LOVE: Ignite The Secret To Your Success*, the second book in *The CODEBREAKER PLATINUM Series*, one story demands to be told.

LOVE IN THE SHOWER

*"Let yourself be silently drawn
by the pull of what you love."*

—*Rumi*

One morning I was in the shower in the front bathroom when a tidal wave of unconditional love filled the whole of my being. I was aware the body was crying and there was no distinction between myself and the shower water. Not only had the water become me and I the water, but in that moment I was everything. I was one with the Divine. There was no separation between who I was and the air, the room, the house, the whole of the universe. I was one with all that is. The True Self had completely annihilated the ego mind's elaborate construct of subject and object, of duality and separation.

I had the vague awareness that my body was still in existence, but I was totally detached from it other than to know that it too was only a tiny particle in the whole of the cosmos, in the mind of the Divine. I was a sublime, drunken puddle of unconditional love merged into God's grace. Unconditional love coursed through the Divine Mind, which had enveloped my mind where nothing else existed. Everything finally disappeared into this love. I was not frightened because fear simply cannot exist in this state, and I had already had similar experiences of being in this state of awe, oneness, and love.

Somehow I had turned off the water and was stepping out of the shower when Daniel walked from his office at the other end of the house into the bathroom. Glowing with joy, he dropped to his knees, tears flowing, overwhelmed by the waves of energy filling the entire apartment emanating from the center of what used to be my being.

He wrapped his arms around my waist, and leaning his head into my wet stomach, he said, "I just tracked down the source of the waves of energy that enveloped me in the most beautiful, unconditional love and total acceptance."

We weren't drunk or on drugs, but we were both drunk and high in the real world of unconditional love where the heart sings with unbridled joy. In this world, forgiveness accomplishes the impossible; all life is unified in all of its beauty and splendor. And this is who we all are; it is our true nature. When you reenter the real world of God, you are perfect beyond the ego mind's ability to comprehend.

When Buddha said, "I am awake," he meant he realized he was not merely a participant in the illusory world of the ego mind but the creator of the entire illusion. This is from one who had become whole in his essence. He woke up to the truth that the world we live in is solely the creation of the ego mind running wild in its dreamlike state.

The love in the shower experience took Daniel and I beyond the realm of our ego minds, and reality moved in on us. When it finally subsided, we were awake to the fact that if it's not Divine love, then it is not real.

"When man learns to experience divine love, he loves himself as a divine manifestation, making unloving behaviors impossible."

—Dr. Valerie Hunt

AFTER THE LOSS

Daniel and I were having lunch with our friends, Bill and Sandy, who had both lost their beloved partners to cancer at least four years previously. In their early 80s, they both looked healthy and vital with a strong, happy life force. There was an air of peace about them that had not necessarily come easily after such tragic losses. Bill and Sandy had known each other for two years, and the pace of their inter-town travels to see each other had not slowed down.

They both have full and exciting lives and are still curious, interested, and eager to learn. You know that makes them incredibly attractive, right? Even before they met each other, they could both have taught us a thing or two about the sexiest trait on the planet. Together, they were dynamic. Their new love and joy was contagious, and the limbic attractors in the brains of the four of us were delightfully stimulated by our subtle energy fields. In other words, the old geezers (as they like to call themselves) were a lot of fun and a pleasure to be around!

Sandy candidly explained without compunction that she had been in such despair after the loss of her husband that she had used antidepressants right up until she met her new love. We had seen and felt the despair of our friend and knew Bill also had a hole in his heart from losing his beloved wife. They had both been through the zombie-like state that makes the world lose all its color, food tasteless, and the happiness of others unfathomable.

Although both Bill and Sandy knew they would never stop loving the ones they had lost, they were smart enough to know there was plenty of room in their huge hearts. Without love, we all feel bereft. Life has no meaning. The world feels like a cruel and empty place.

When trauma strikes, such as the death of someone very close to you, a major illness, a divorce, or loss of your job, the pain is great. If your ego mind convinces you that you have a legitimate reason to believe someone else has contributed to your pain, it then becomes excruciating. The normal response is to ask, "Why me?" Then, to become angry. Then, to throw yourself into other areas and activities.

If the trauma and resentment or guilt is severe enough, there is still a major wound that must be healed before peace and love can be restored. This is often referred to as "a hole in the heart." The ego mind is quick to take advantage of all this suffering. Programs surface like, "What's the point?" "I am all alone in the world; no one understands what I'm going through!" "I've lost everything, life is not worth living." "No one cares about me, I may as well give up and die!"

Have you ever met anyone who has felt that way? You might have even asked yourself those questions in times of despair. Frequently, the person suffering from this feels that nothing can fill the hole in their heart and continues on a downward spiral, battling what is an invisible foe. The ego mind's unconscious stories are the invisible enemy.

In other words, your programs are the problem. And even if you do not sink into depression, experience other mental and/or physical problems, or resort to drugs, alcohol, sex or food addictions and abuse, with the help from the ego mind the hole in the heart remains. Peace has not been attained and love has not been restored.

THE HOLE IN THE HEART CAN BE MADE TO DISAPPEAR

The most effective way of closing the hole is to eliminate it entirely. Clearly, enlightened forgiveness is the surest and most effective way to accomplish this. In fact, it may be the only way to restore peace and create a new foundation of Love.

Peace and love are the bedrock of being able to live a PLATINUM life. When the soul chooses the Divine Mind as its guide you evolve into the best version of you, moving up and across on the Integrated Wholeness Scale. Life really is not worth living below 200 on this map of the evolution of your soul. It is only when you sit squarely at 500—at love or above—that we quiet and transcend the ego mind's questions, and life becomes that crazy good experience it was always meant to be.

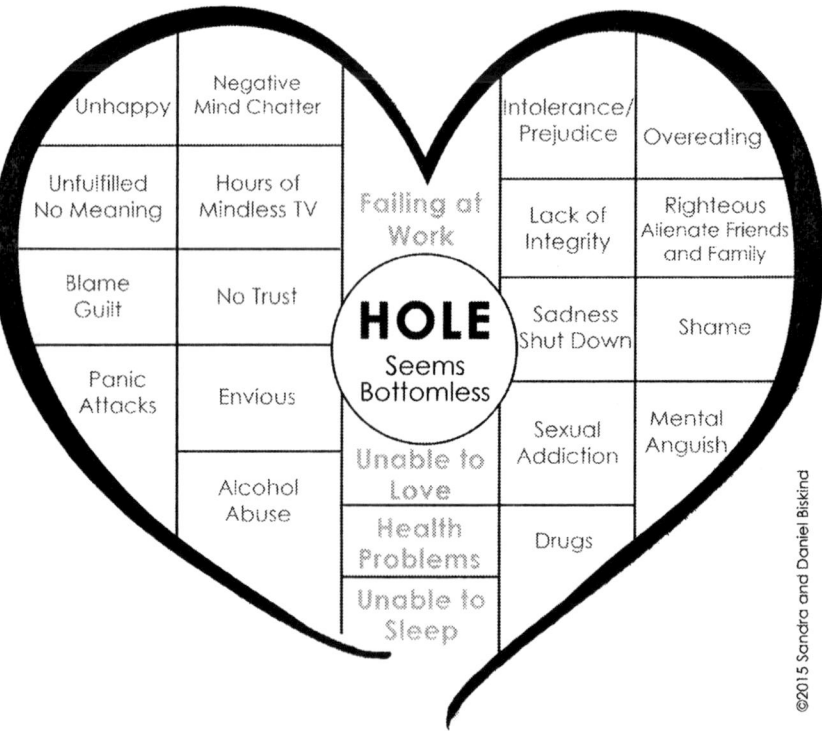

LOVE: IGNITE THE SECRET TO YOUR SUCCESS

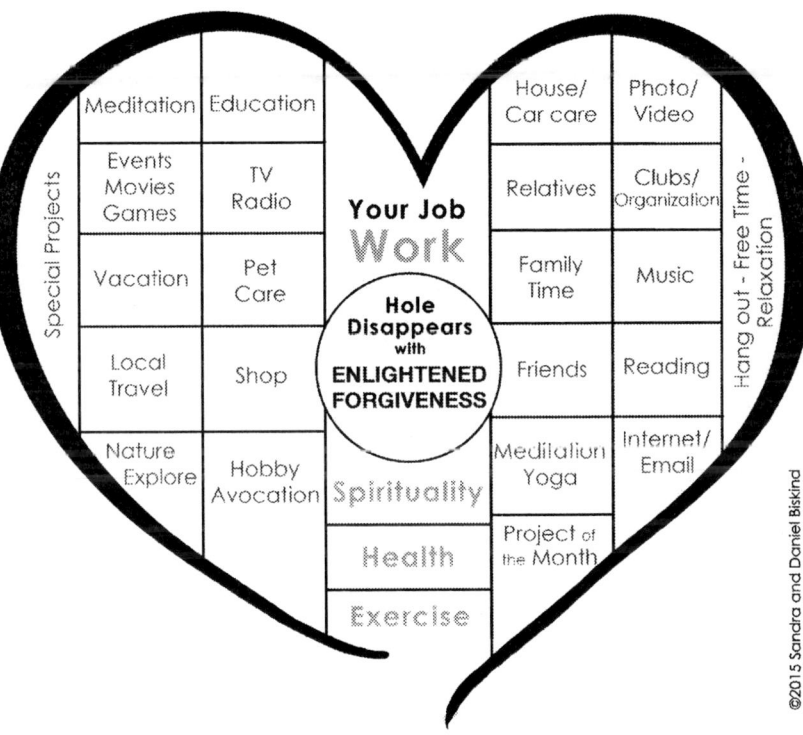

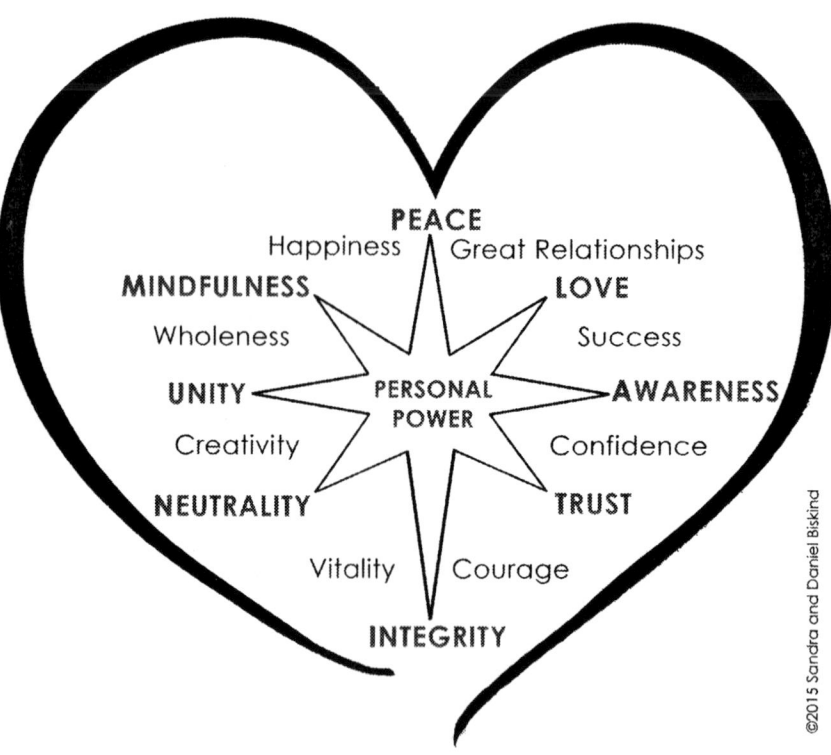

LOVE: THE UNDERESTIMATED GENIUS OF THE HEART

At your core, love is who you are—and the genius of the heart knows no boundaries. It has no limit on how many people can come into its orbit and be safe there. Your capacity to express more of what your primordial nature is cannot be contained, measured, or put in a box. Only in the ego mind's illusory world do you need to pigeonhole love. Our wise friends, Bill and Sandy, clearly understood that only love could mend their broken hearts—pure genius!

Another one of my best friends just turned 98. She, too, lost her husband many years ago, but because of her deep spiritual awareness, she has never been alone or without love.

When we walk into her house we have to make a path for ourselves through all the angels and divine beings who drop in and out at her invitation. She knows she is loved and looked after and at 2 years shy of 100, she still has the air of a mischievous Irish imp. She sits in her tiny apartment with her magnetic personal power radiating out from the depth of her spiritual core. The love, peace, and joy we feel every time we are with her brings us closer to our own personal power and enhances our connection to our Divine Mind Code. As one of Daniel's children said after meeting her for the first time, "I just wanted to crawl up into a ball and lay at her feet for the rest of my life!"

> *"Neither a lofty degree of intelligence
> nor imagination nor both together
> go to the making of genius.
> Love, love, love,
> that is the soul of genius."*
>
> —Wolfgang Amadeus Mozart

LOVE AT ONE HUNDRED AND SIX

I really loved this wonderful story about the genius of the soul when it chooses love. In a two-page spread in a local paper in my hometown, there was a full-page photo of a man and woman together with the heading, "Love at One Hundred and Six." They had met two years ago in the retirement village where they both lived. She was 106 and he was 79. They had decided not to get married because they had not married their previous partners, so why start now? He said she was the smartest, funniest, and most wise woman he had ever met. They were radiant!

> *"The heart has its reasons whereof reason knows nothing."*
>
> —Blaise Pascal

The people in the stories above were not looking for people to be space fillers. They chose to activate their capacity to love, even through adversity, and were genuinely and positively transformed.

Everyone comes into relationships full of hope. Even with your most beloved family members you can still wonder why you end up in so much pain so often. Remember, the ego mind has hijacked you over many lifetimes. We all have programs that continually warn us how dangerous it can be to love and how futile or even disempowering it is to forgive and let go.

Without mastering the art of forgiveness, your relationships quickly fall by the wayside, only to be replaced by more of the same. Have you ever watched anyone go through a series of relationships, one right after another, and still end up with the same partner but in a different package? People become space fillers and space fillers are easy to replace.

Einstein defined insanity as doing the same thing over and over again and expecting different results.

Forgiveness is such a big decision it affects the whole world. The first person you must forgive is yourself. Until you experience the infinite love of the real world, it is easy to dupe yourself into believing that you are just a body and that whatever is happening is your lot in life and that you are relatively powerless to change it. But that is not the truth.

You have the power within you to change the way you think and feel about any situation.

Humanity lives on this glorious planet that is so bountiful and filled with so much beauty, yet like a small child accepts its parents' authority as truthful, we fail to question the content of an ego mind that continues to imprison us via its thoughts, ideas, and beliefs, which we mistakenly believe to be our own.

Our programs condition us and act like prison bars and chains that have us shut tight in our own little world. Far be it for anyone to challenge what the ego mind believes to be true. It automatically rejects ideas foreign to its experience of life and readily finds others guilty of disagreeing with it, imprisoning them in cells even smaller than our own.

> *"A man should look for what is, and not for what he thinks should be."*
>
> —*Albert Einstein*

Have you ever experienced that uneasy feeling that comes after you have been talking negatively about another person? Once you have played at being judge and jury over yourself and others, you are still not happy and wonder why. Did you know that when you judge another person, your unconscious mind applies that same judgment to you? This is why the saying, "When you point a finger at someone else, there are three pointing back at you," is true not only physically but psychologically as well.

When you use the Master Password to set yourself free, you access the Divine Mind Code which facilitates becoming neutral, dissolving the bars of your self-created prison.

Use the information mystics and scientists alike offer you about the workings of the body, brain, and heart to help you realize your full potential. Break free of the ego mind code that keeps its prison doors tightly locked, walking in circles of self-righteousness with little joy and not much love. It is as simple as choosing these eight, power-packed keywords: Peace, Love, Awareness, Trust, Integrity, Neutrality, Unity, and Mindfulness.

OPEN SESAME

Like Aladdin's password that led him into the cave to the bottle with the genie who granted him three wishes, PLATINUM is your abracadabra and your open sesame.

The Divine Mind Code encompasses enlightenment, forgiveness, and every concept contained in the Master Password. It is the bottle with the magical, wish-granting genie, except here you get unlimited wishes. You simply must decide to get out of the prison of belief and into the treasure trove of the real world where infinite love, compassion, kindness, and your perfect point of power reside.

There are two primary motivating forces in conflict with each other on the prison planet and they are not about race, religion, or politics. Love and fear collide, and without love, fear reigns supreme. The sneaky thing about fear is that it is often unconscious. Whenever you are not in an aware state, it is likely to sneak up and slap you around before you even know what has hit you.

On the other side of fear you will find the best version of you.

PAINFUL GAMES

When you find yourself saying and doing painful things that are out of character, you may wonder, "Where did that come from?" When someone hurts you, it is easy to go in to shock, unable to fathom how they could do or say such hurtful things. It's no surprise that you have conveniently forgotten all the times you have been guilty of the same cruelty.

Three young girls—all about seven or eight years old and all dressed up with just-washed, shiny, long hair—were having a night out at the movie theater. They were waiting for their parents outside the cinema complex, and as we walked toward them, we overheard their conversation. Two of them were taunting the third girl, telling her they no longer wanted her around. While the other two linked arms and smugly walked away, her little face dropped, the fun and enthusiasm of only moments before completely forgotten.

We had to walk past them on the way to our car, and I said in a very soft, non-judgmental voice, "Don't be cruel, girls." One of them guiltily replied, "We were only playing a game." I said, "Yes, but even games can hurt." As we reached the car, we saw the three girls together again and heard the one who had spoken to me say to her friends, "Where did she come from?" as though we had beamed down from out of nowhere.

Open the doors, break out of the prison cell, and walk into the light of a higher awareness dialogue. Which one are you drawn to? The one that perpetuates your cruel games, or the voice that comes from out of nowhere and frees you to love again?

The unconscious mind is where your learned behaviors, beliefs, and ideas—whether useful or destructive—are stored. Until the compromised software programs are neutralized on the hard drive of your human computer, the resultant fears and games they cause you to play will wreak havoc in your life. Then, the war within you manifests as war in the outer world, be it about race or religion, politics or power, gender or culture.

Fear is simply the manifestation of the mind's corrupted software programs, whereas love is the manifestation of the Divine Heart in action. Only love is capable of unlocking the doors to a life filled with happiness and eternal joy.

"No one is born hating another person
because of the color of his skin,
or his background, or his religion.
People must learn to hate,
and if they can learn to hate,
they can be taught to love,
for love comes more naturally
to the human heart
than its opposite."

Long Walk to Freedom:
The Autobiography of Nelson Mandela

THE SCIENCE OF LOVE

Science and medicine are continually learning more about how the wonderful tools we call the body and the brain operate. Their insights help us develop new ways to unlock the ego mind code so we can work with the neurophysiology of the brain to reprogram, neutralize, and delete unconscious fears and other destructive emotions that are so easily triggered in the absence of love.

A General Theory of Love by Thomas Lewis, M.D., Fari Amini, M.D., and Richard Lannon, M.D. explains in elegant prose how the brain works and its relationship to love. It is a great read! To quote from these wonderful doctors who are delving into the mystical world of the heart from a scientific perspective, "In all cases, emotions are humanity's motivator and it's omnipresent guide."

When they talk about all of the benefits of cognition and the brilliance of the human intellect and all of the ways they have made our lives easier—from plumbing to the game changer of the Internet—they say, "But even as it reaps the benefits of reason, modern America plows emotions under—a costly practice that obstructs happiness and misleads people about the nature and significance of their lives."

They tell us that science has discovered emotion's deeper purpose. "The timeworn mechanisms of emotions allow two human beings to receive the contents of each other's minds. Emotion is the messenger of love; it is the signal that carries one brimming heart to another."

However, repressed or unresolved emotion is the messenger of fear. It is the signal that carries one shattered, imprisoned mind to another.

Love is the genie with the promise of granting us the inner strength and power to get off the roller coaster ride of negative life patterns, to unshackle the shattered heart and restore it to wholeness. It is the precious gift of your True Self hidden deep within your heart.

> *"**Love is a magician. Everything it touches turns into itself.**"*
>
> —P. Wilson

TRANSCENDENT VIBRATIONS

Valerie Hunt, Ph.D. explains in her book *Infinite Mind: Science of the Human Vibrations of Consciousness* explains, "Some aspects of reality—the mind is one—cannot be explained in a material framework. Mind has energy since it causes things to happen. Many of the experiences that we casually attribute to the mind are clearly brain functions: reflexes and responses to material reality that are recorded in and recovered from the brain. Other experiences and capacities such as thought, insight, imagination, and soul seem to be properties of the higher mind."

Dr. Hunt is talking about what we term super consciousness, our faculty that accesses the Divine Mind. Nobel Prize-winning neurophysiologist Sir John Eccles said during a series of lectures at Harvard, "The unity of conscious experience comes from a self-conscious mind, not from a neural mechanism of the neocortex. The evolutionary process can account for the brain, but only something transcendent could explain consciousness and thought."

Here we have cutting-edge scientific minds of our time moving beyond conventional thinking into the lofty heights of coming to grips with reality. The brain is the super computer that stores and processes the information that the mind gives it. It stores all information without judgment or bias. They are teaching you the importance of being able to master your mind. You are the programmer of your life codes, and you are the one who has to decipher those codes long after the physical brain has lost the key and forgotten the passwords.

We will delve into this subject in greater depth in the next book, *AWARENESS: Discover How Life Really Works.*

Divine Love is infinite, unconditional, and all-encompassing. It surpasses the understanding of the logical mind and opens the door to the health and well-being of your body, mind, and soul. It is the prerequisite to the miracle of real forgiveness and the joy that comes from knowing you can move on from the darkness—the guilt, shame, and blame of your ego mind's programs—and do what you love, and love what you do.

PAST, PRESENT, AND FUTURE PROGRAMS

We worked with a man named Jonathan who had been sexually abused by his uncle as a child, and then had gone on to abuse his little sister in later years. He was in real torment. A black hole of shame had been sucking all the joy from his life ever since both events. Although he had talked it over with his sister many times, and she had forgiven him, he could not find it in himself to do the same. Even though he thought he had forgiven his uncle, it was only his head that had done so.

He was in his early 30s and had been searching for relief through books and seminars for many years before he came to one of our events. He honestly thought that happiness and loving relationships were beyond his reach. He committed to spending a week-long Intensive working with us, and toward the end of the week, he was so immersed in his heart that he truly forgave his uncle. He could no longer feel the anger surrounding the abuse. All despair was nowhere to be found.

However, Jonathan's thoughts about his sister continued to trigger the deep wounds still wrapped with the acid of the shame he had been carrying for decades. On the last day of the Intensive, we resumed with the part of the process that everyone looked forward to every day, which the participants dubbed Story Time. Everyone took a turn in the hot seat, which was the chair beside mine, where a personal transformational story from a parallel, past, present, or alternate life was revealed to them.

ALTERNATIVE LIVES?

At this point, it is important to say that it is not necessary to believe in past or parallel lives. Dr. Brian Weiss, an eminent psychiatrist, successfully uses hypnotically-induced past-life therapy as a technique for dealing with emotional and physical problems in this lifetime. We access alternative lives as a tool to help discover core programs that act like viruses in your operating system and stop you from being able to access your personal power—the best version of you. We get results and people's lives change dramatically for the better when these core programs have been corrected from their operating system.

Humans are hardwired for stories. In our work, we consider these stories to be similar to Jungian archetypes or classic, timeless myths that have profound personal significance for you. There is no need to believe in alternative lives for this technique to be effective.

All information has specific frequencies. Using the correct frequencies neutralizes the emotional charge around information, transforming it from a controlling program to merely benign data in your data bank. Just ask yourself, "Would I rather be right or be happy?" When you answer "happy," you can open your mind to new ways of thinking and being to have the life you want.

The participants in this Intensive had already been through past and future life meditations that had uncovered the sources of programs that needed to be corrected. It was obvious how these unconscious programs were still playing out in their lives in destructive life patterns. In the hot-seat process, they became neutral to the emotions, decisions, and judgments surrounding these events that had been unconsciously controlling them.

Moving forward in their relationships, jobs, and the physical world became easier. People were freed to make new choices that could now come from the innate wisdom and creativity of the heart. We were all more able to tap into our personal power and move forward in the world with real strength and freedom. The Story Time process facilitated instant transformation in the life of every member of the group.

One high-powered business executive, a woman in her early 40s, changed so much when she moved from her head into her heart that she found—to her amazement and the amazement of her staff—that after being disliked for years, she was liked and respected at last. The new woman that emerged from within her changed her relationships so dynamically that the whole company prospered.

Jonathan, who had been unable to forgive himself, at last found peace as he was finally able to let go of his shame and the unhappiness that held him hostage to despair.

While everyone's eyes were closed during the visualization, I wrote on the white board a new mantra that clinched the deal for him. The big "aha" moment came when he read, "No matter what you have or have not said or done, you still deserve love." When Jonathan came out of the forgiveness meditation and absorbed the quote on the white board, his whole demeanor dramatically changed. The penny finally dropped. His stubborn ego mind that had imprisoned him with guilt was finally knocked on its head. His prison break changed his life.

Jonathan was finally neutral to the events, emotions, and decisions that had kept him in a loop of guilt, shame, and blame. He floated out of the Intensive on an invisible energy field of infinite, unconditional love. His body looked stronger and more alive. A wide and wonderful smile on his face made him look more his age—younger, and more attractive. These are just a few examples of the typical results we have grown to expect when working with the unexpected genius of the heart.

"The best and most beautiful things in the world cannot be seen or even touched—they must be felt with the heart."

—Helen Keller

THE HAPPINESS FACTOR

During our Intensives, people are often on a high in a peak state of awareness that is classically associated with enlightenment. In this state, happiness becomes a deep well of joy, and it can be impossible not to let the face know about it. A smile can heal an ailing heart, it can uplift a grieving soul, and it automatically changes the way you feel. It is hard to stay unhappy when you smile.

As one of the 20th century's great philosophers, Charles Schultz, portrayed in his cartoon of Charlie Brown, a smile can change your world. Charlie Brown was bent over at the waist facing the ground when Lucy came up to him and asked him, "What are you doing?" He said, "I'm being depressed." He then stood up straight and smiled and said, "Because if I stand up straight like this and smile, I won't feel depressed anymore!"

On the inner journey out of the darkness and into the light of Divine Love, we learn a wonderful truth:

The key to enlightenment is to lighten up.

Your million-dollar expression of delight, love, sincerity, courage, success, welcome, and acceptance can be seen in the power of your smile. When you have slipped out of your heart, like Charlie Brown, make the conscious choice to stand up straight and smile. Not only is it hard to stay unhappy, but if you savor your smile deeply, it becomes difficult to remember what caused the slip in the first place.

Another advantage is that other people usually respond to a smile in positive ways, often despite themselves. You are not seen as a threat when you smile, and you never know when someone needs the warmth of a smile just to feel better for an instant. It costs you nothing to smile and to bring the light of love into your often dark and scary world; it only pays dividends.

When children smile, it comes from their hearts and it is full of genuine joy. They smile up to 400 times a day. As an adult, you are lucky if you get 15 smiles on your face in a day. When you share a smile, it reassures children and adults alike that they are okay and that their world is a safe place.

Daniel and I have had fun traveling to the ends of the earth exploring our own spirituality. We've learned that wherever you go—there you are! Right now, right where you are, you can tap into that place of divine love within you that gives you the strength to stand up straight and smile.

Enlightenment is a state of causeless love and limitless joy. It has a happiness factor to it that cannot be denied, and why would you? In the words of the globally popular song by Pharrell Williams, "Happiness Is the Truth."

THE NEED FOR LOVING FAMILY CONNECTIONS

Scientists have developed the field of computational neuroscience in the quest to understand the workings of the human brain. In the process, they have discovered that love alters the physical structure of your brain. How much love you did or did not receive from your parents and extended family is one of the key determinants of the way your brain functions, along with the programs by which your subconscious mind operates.

Your destiny as a well-adjusted, intelligent, socially-skilled, loving person is powerfully influenced by what you hear and feel in your mother's voice and life experience while in the womb. Even before birth, the mind's observations are processed at lightening speed. Like a sponge, your brain is operating at the programming levels of theta and delta, and you are absorbing and filing information with no filters to inform you if something is real or true.

Humans, like all mammals, are hardwired with a strong family instinct. The development of a child is directly linked to the mother, her programs, and the experiences the mother had since the child's conception. The hurricane of violence that is spreading throughout youth in America and the whole world is symptomatic of a lack of love, and it underscores the importance of the role of family in the lives of our beautiful babies. Is it too late to reach those who appear to be lost?

With patient, loving mentoring, we can help bring about changes in the choices made by our corrupted youth. They have been hog-tied by the ego mind's unconscious drive for its version of love and fulfillment. Hungrily looking for some form of happiness, they form pack-like gangs where they become members of a family where they pretend to be safe.

*"I refuse to accept the view
that mankind is so tragically bound
to the starless midnight of racism
and war that the bright daybreak
of peace and brotherhood
can never become a reality...
I believe that unarmed truth
and unconditional love
will have the final word."*

–Martin Luther King, Jr.

AN ANCIENT PARABLE FOR TODAY

A woman came out of her house and saw three old men with long white beards sitting in her front yard. She did not recognize them. She said "I don't think I know you, but you must be hungry. Please come in and have something to eat."

"Is the man of the house home?" they asked.

"No," she replied "He's out."

"Then we cannot come in," they replied.

In the evening, when her husband came home, she told him what had happened.

"Go tell them I am home and invite them in!"

The woman went out and invited the men in.

"We do not go into a house together," they replied.

"Why is that?" she asked.

One of the old men explained: "His name is Wealth," he said pointing to one of his friends, and said pointing to the other man, "He is Success, and I am Love." Then he added, "Now go in and discuss with your husband which one of us you want in your home."

The woman went in and told her husband what was said. Her husband was overjoyed. "How nice!" he said. "Since that is the case let us invite in Wealth. Let him come in and fill our home with wealth!"

His wife disagreed. "My dear, why don't we invite Success?"

Their daughter-in-law was listening from the other corner of the house. She jumped in with her own suggestion: "Would it not be better to invite Love? Our home will then be filled with love!"

"Let us heed our daughter-in-law's advice," said the husband to his wife.

"Go out and invite Love to be our guest."

The woman went out and asked the three old men, "Which one of you is Love? Please come in and be our guest."

Love got up and started to walk toward the house. The other two men got up and followed him. Surprised, the woman asked Wealth and Success, "I only invited Love; why are you coming in?"

The old men replied together, "If you had invited Wealth and Success, the other two of us would have stayed outside, but since you invited Love, wherever he goes, we go with him. Wherever there is Love, there is also Wealth and Success!"

NEURONS FIRING ON ALL CYLINDERS

"Let the beauty we love be what we do."

—*Rumi*

With neurons firing on all cylinders when you perceive beauty, you attain a state of creative appreciation, bypassing the ego mind in that moment, taking you into the Divine Mind and the Divine Heart. I have always verbalized my love for everything — people, animals, places. To me, everything translates into art in some form. Once, I sat literally shaking at the wheel of my parked car after having just spent three hours buying a fashion range for my boutiques. The designer had put together a collection of clothes which was so impressive that every item was like a work of art.

My whole being, every cell, was vibrating with excitement at having spent the whole afternoon surrounded by such a fantastic collection. Neurons were definitely firing on all cylinders, and creativity was at an all-time high as I saw how the clothes would look in my boutiques and how I would display them so my clients could best appreciate them. I knew exactly what they would look like on my customers and how excited they would be. It was such a high.

I was passionate about the range, the work I was doing, and how great this collection was. I knew every other woman would also feel confident and alive when they wore them. You could say I was in love. That is what it feels like when you are living from a state of appreciation, and you perceive the wonder around you. When your focus is not just on yourself but on how you can serve others, it is usually a sign you have stepped into your personal power and are in success mode.

And yes, it was one of the most successful collections I had ever bought. For one of my boutiques I bought over three times the amount that the designer had bought for her own three stores, and I was still calling for as much as she would give me during the season.

The high of loving the art form translated into the high of success!

> *"You will find as you look back upon your life that the moments when you have truly lived are the moments when you have done things in the spirit of love."*
>
> —Henry Drummond

THE CODEBREAKER SUCCESS FREQUENCY

This is one of the most critical components we discuss when coaching business executives and sales people. You are the CEO and COO of your own life. This applies to everyone, regardless of your job.

First, get your thinking right by neutralizing obstacles to success and self-esteem issues. Commit to being of service in whatever way possible. Always having your mind on the ball and the players at the same time reaps huge rewards for you, your employees, and your customers. Love what you do and the people you do it with.

Get onto the success frequency. At the very least, find something you can be passionate about in what you do now. Until your soul chooses to realign yourself with your True Self, your ego mind programs will sabotage your success.

The easiest way to ignite the secret to your success is to know with every fiber of your being that love is who you are. That love does not come from the illusory world the ego mind created to perpetuate fear and separation. The highest form of love is spiritual love which operates by the Divine Mind Code. It recognizes the Divinity not only in you, but in every living being.

When you allow your programs to run rampant, it is easy for your human computer to crash and burn. It is easy to sit in judgment of yourself and others and begin wars that bring your personal world into chaos and despair. Spiritual love is the water that quenches your thirst, frees you from the isolation of separation, and magnetizes even more love into your life. This love does not expect anything in return and is whole unto itself—and just think, this is who you are!

This love that is your essential nature is and always will be hardwired as who you are. No matter what circumstances have transpired, no matter what programs you have been running as unconscious software from childhood or societal conditioning, love is who you always have been and always will be.

This is the stuff of miracles. Daniel and I had been frequenting a little cafe in a seaside resort town for a few months and had become friendly with the chef and all the staff. The day before we were to leave town, one of the servers brought us our coffees and almost broke down as she placed the cups on our table. She was a beautiful young girl of about 17. With tears in her eyes, she looked at us and said, "What is it? I always feel so good when you are here. What are you doing?"

"Love. We just love you, that's all." With that, the tears made tracks down her cheeks as she looked at us and said, "I thought so. It's just I have never felt love like this before, and I have never been happier than I have been recently. Thank you. I know my life has changed because you have loved me."

Before that day, we had never told this girl we loved her, but her life was positively affected by the vibrational match she was feeling to the energy of love. The frequency of love is enough to change your life and the life of anyone in its orbit who is ready to become the best version of themselves.

Know this, even if your ego mind objects violently:

The frequency of love is the frequency of success.

You might just need to get neutral again here!

I once allowed a young man, with whom I was very impressed at the time, to tell me I should not say I "love" things. Little did I know, as an impressionable 16-year old, that he was telling me to have one of my greatest gifts stand down. It was no wonder I had a mini meltdown during our relationship. Ever since I can remember, the child who had always loved so fully and who had received Divine guidance to express and be love, was trying to conform to another's idea of what love should be.

It did not work for me, and needless to say, neither did the relationship. I continue to love indiscriminately and have found a partner whose success in life also comes about by keeping his heart in his brave hands and continuing to love regardless.

With that love as your baseline, you are mindful of your feelings and aware of the needs and desires of others, and no matter how much pain is involved in any relationship, you stay true to one definitive dictate:

Love no matter what. Forgive when given the chance. Become ever-vigilant to any judgments that drop in, and drop them like hotcakes.

Remain mindful of how you are choosing to feel and how the wonder of your world affects you. Love is the frequency of success, and it is who you are. The only thing stopping you from staying on the frequency of love and having the life you want is your ego mind.

Use this simple process to stay attuned to the success frequency of LOVE:

Whenever you are feeling fear, negativity, shame, blame, guilt, or pain, ask yourself, "When did I start to feel like this?"

Track your thoughts back to the source. It might not necessarily have been a major challenge; it could have been something quite innocent that triggered an ego mind program that set off your emotional response.

For example you might have seen an attractive person and thought, "They would never love me." Programs like, I'm not good enough, smart enough, funny enough, or beautiful enough are triggered at lightening speed and at the same speed you have moved away from your perfect point of power, which is the frequency of love.

Once you have pinpointed the program, you can neutralize it and delete its effects by using The Quantum Neutrality Process. You can also use True Self Reprogramming.

TRUE SELF REPROGRAMMING

- Clear yourself by thumping your thymus (tapping your breastbone) and thinking of someone or something you love.

- Having identified the offending program, e.g. "I am not worthy of love," look into your eyes in a mirror and from your heart say, "My True Self is perfect. I am worthy of love because love is who I am. I am in perfect harmony with the energy of love."

- Create new neural pathways by repeating the positive attributes of love for one minute every few hours for one month.

This process works to balance your whole being—mentally, emotionally, physically, spiritually, and psychologically. Whether you have been passed up for a job promotion, your relationship has failed, a friend has let you down, a family member has hurt you, or you just don't believe in yourself, use the True Self Reprogramming statements, "My True Self is perfect. I am worthy of love because love is who I am. I am in perfect harmony with the energy of love," as powerful reminders of your true essence.

Nothing outside yourself can satisfy your longing for love like your True Self can.

The truth is that you have always been worthy of love; you have always been beautiful enough, strong enough, smart enough. You can attune yourself to the frequency of love at any time. Like a prayer these statements form an energy that you send out to the cosmos aligning yourself with the Divine Mind Code.

Be your own best friend. Love yourself the way you can only imagine the Divine Mind loves you—fully and completely. As the most powerful magnetic force in the universe, love attracts miracles into your life. Connect fully to the love that you are and unleash the immeasurable power of the Divine Mind. The irresistible magnetic influence of love knows no boundaries.

Change your thoughts. Love is not something you have to get, give, or do.

Change your life. Love is the awesome, profoundly fundamental, and essential energy that is who you are. You are what you have been looking for.

Change your world. Be the love you want to see in the world, and your world will become a vibrational match to the energy of love.

Continue to be a mirror for the love that others are, even if they have programs acting as obstacles to that love.

When you express the love that you are, you give others permission to do the same.

To paraphrase Michael Jackson, if you want to make the world a better place, take a look at yourself, and then make the change you want to see.

> "Miracles occur naturally
> as expressions of love.
> The real miracle is the love
> that inspires them.
> In this sense everything
> that comes from love
> is a miracle."
>
> —*A Course in Miracles*

A MEDITATION ON LOVE: IGNITE THE SECRET TO YOUR SUCCESS

Center yourself by taking a few deep breaths and align yourself to a frequency of peace. Begin by observing your breath and letting your body relax. Let go of all judgments as you allow your thoughts to simply come and go.

Say to yourself, *"Love is my essence. My True Self is the perfect expression of God, of love, peace, and joy."* Continue to breathe deeply as your whole being makes the shift to this powerful vibrational frequency of love. Just as darkness is displaced by light, in this moment your ego mind's programs are transformed; fear, pride, worry, guilt, and shame have been displaced by love.

Strengthen your body by using your imagination to see, feel, touch, or know someone you love sitting opposite you. It could even be your beloved pet.

With all your heart, say, *"I love you."* Bask in the feeling of being this love. It has no conditions. There is nothing either of you need to do, get, or give. The Divine Mind has taken center stage for this act, and you are the star in the middle of the most awesome love scene ever written.

Take your awareness into your soul and say, *"I choose to live the love that I am."* Then look into the eyes of the one you love and say, *"Thank you for aligning me with the love that I am."*

Now imagine a column of white light pouring into your head and filling your body right down to your feet and toes. This is the light of your True Self that you have accessed by changing your thoughts to love. Allow this white light to flow freely, getting hotter and stronger as you stay aware of your breath, your body still relaxing even more.

With every breath you take, your body, mind, and soul are being regenerated, rejuvenated, strengthened, and renewed. The love that you are is your pathway to success. You have now ignited the secret to your success to better relationships, more vitality, expanded creativity, and the ability to direct your soul to choose to stay in this place of trust, presence, and strength; to live in the real world of the Divine.

Stay in this expanded place, basking in the love that you are for as long as you can. You can also bring other people into your meditation on love. Once you have totally aligned with this unfathomably rich place of unity with your source and the cosmos, you are free to bring into your meditation someone who has hurt you.

When you have them before you, imagine the same white light coursing through you also enveloping them from head to toe. Once again, say, *"Love is my essence. My True Self is the perfect expression of God, of love, peace, and joy."* Then look at the person opposite you and say. *"I love you. Thank you for aligning me with the love that I am."*

Engage your imagination even further and take a moment to feel the other person relax, breathe easier and match up their vibration of love to yours. Now say, *"I forgive all my programs that have separated us and I forgive all your programs that have hurt me."*

The whole world has just taken a deep breath! Real forgiveness is the natural expression of love, of God, of the Divine Mind.

When you are ready, take a few more deep breaths and slowly open your eyes. You are now in tune with the high vibration of love. This powerful exercise has activated the best version of you. Share it with the world. Stay on this frequency for as long as you can.

If you feel yourself slipping into fear, negativity, or pain, reignite the high frequency of love with this meditation and imagine yourself as the person you are loving and forgiving.

EGO PUPPY TRAINING #2: LOVE

If you have not read *PEACE: Power Up Your Life*, the first book in The CODEBREAKER PLATINUM Series, you have missed Ego Puppy Training #1.

In it, we asked you to have some fun and imagine your ego mind is your new puppy. Its name, of course, is Ego Puppy. It has already learned some terrible tricks from the rest of the litter, the untrained mother, and the mostly-absent father. When you first bring it home, you are convinced it has been roaming wild for centuries.

Your Ego Puppy has already displayed its discontent by whining and crying through the confusion of not having its basic survival needs met. It then goes into despair, which is a natural response when you have lost something as precious as love. Through the most important learning phase, the children unlucky enough to have ignorant, unloving parents learn that they do not really matter, they are not worthy of love, and they are responsible for all the misfortune that befalls them.

Even coming from the most loving parents, it is hard to navigate through the illusory world the ego mind creates. It is almost impossible for the abused Ego Puppy.

Without love, they wither and die inside to the feelings of the rest of the world. Why should they have empathy for others and treat them well when that has not been their experience?

These Ego Puppies of the world become a whole new species. They are by far the most dangerous animal on this planet, both to themselves and to others. The younger puppies can growl and gnaw with their baby teeth without dangerous consequences. However, if you ignore the signs and omit the training, the puppy very quickly grows into a vicious dog.

In this illusory world, we feel the danger and typically only see the viciousness without looking into the heart of the matter. Our ego minds are these Ego Puppies, and they are capable of anything in their corrupted cries for love and attention. Everything that happens can be understood to be an opportunity to forgive and to find your way back to love. This is at the heart of the training we all need.

Look into your heart to see if you have truly forgiven your parents, siblings, and friends for having hurt you. Find the love that resides within you that may or may not have been nurtured as a child. Your mission, if you choose to accept it, is to nurture this love—first for yourself, and then for others. Express this love wherever possible, and neutralize any program that would sabotage fulfilling your mission.

"Life has taught us that love does not consist of gazing at each other, but in looking outward together in the same direction."

—Antoine de Saint-Exupery

JUMPSTART THE PROCESS

"Man is a credulous animal and must believe something. In the absence of good grounds for belief, he will be satisfied with bad ones."

—Bertrand Russell

The CODEBREAKER PLATINUM Series presents a systematic process that you can adapt to suit your own needs and lifestyle to power up your life. It contains a wide range of simple tools, techniques, and practices that all complement and reinforce one another. They fall into the two categories which encompass all fundamental approaches to inner development in every spiritual and personal development tradition: inquiry and attunement.

INQUIRY practices are those in which you ask yourself questions.

ATTUNEMENT practices are those in which you harmonize your own frequency with a frequency of your choice.

INQUIRY: To start, we present three simple but powerful inquiry techniques: The Four Questions, Rate Your State, and the Quantum Neutrality Process. Empowered neutrality is where you consistently correct emotional blocks that stop you from living the best version of you. To get you started we have outlined the first easy steps so you can correct emotional blocks and go from feeling awful to awesome in minutes.

ATTUNEMENT: Reading this series of books attunes you to the enlightenment frequency as does working with us at our live events and digital programs. Another attunement practice we strongly recommend is meditation. We offer you a link to a free guided meditation on our website www.TheBiskinds.com, which you are welcome to download and use as often as you can.

We suggest using it at least once daily.

The more you use these tools, the more you will get from them. Not only will you become more skillful in their use, but their impact is cumulative.

This is an introduction to a lifelong system that can take you as far and as deep and as high on the Integrated Wholeness Scale as you are prepared to go. Have fun! And remember, your thoughts are the only thing stopping you from having the life you want.

THE FOUR QUESTIONS: LOVE

This inquiry technique utilizes your internal GPS.

It is based on the use of mindfulness, which is simply observing yourself without judgment. It is self-awareness. This powerful exercise cultivates your emotional intelligence.

Use your feelings as your readout on your internal GPS. The more negative you are feeling, the more off course you are. The better you feel, the more on course you are. Making repeated course corrections is an easy and effective way to change your state.

Use it to connect with your true north, your True Self.

This simple set of questions will change the way you feel from one moment to the next. As you practice and become proficient, this technique will become second nature and you will use it like auto-pilot to course-correct automatically.

Use it whenever you feel yourself moving away from your natural state of peace and love. Recognize that it is only untrained ego mind mischief at play.

Answer the questions truthfully and spontaneously. Stay focused on the answer to question number four for as long as you can.

This is an example only. Use your own words and the wisdom of your own heart to answer these questions.

1. **What am I feeling?**
   I feel lonely and afraid.

2. **What am I focused on?**
   Being alone.

3. **How do I want to feel?**
   Happy and loved.

4. **What focus will serve that?**
   Being grateful for all the creativity, passion, and love I have in my life right now.

As you relax and center yourself, reconnect with the love that you are. That takes fear and desperation out of the equation. You will shift into a place of wholeness and personal power, a place that is incredibly attractive to everyone. It is the state in which you are mindful not to place expectations on others.

RATE YOUR STATE: LOVE

Use these three questions to guide you into experiencing more love in your life. You might need to change your codes depending on the answers.

1) Do you train your mind to think thoughts of love and forgiveness, constantly moving you in the direction of a peaceful, loving mind?

The ego mind is quick to make everyone and everything wrong. Pay attention to how your thoughts are creating pain or joy. Train the ego mind to align with the perfection of your True Self. The miracles of forgiveness, acceptance, and tolerance bring you back into your heart, back into love, and higher on the Integrated Wholeness Scale.

2) When was the last time you continued to love someone even after they hurt you?

The ego mind has given the people you love the greatest power to press your buttons and bring up feelings of anger and despair. Discover your programs that gave their programs this power over your feelings. Neutralize them, and delete their power. You will rise to love and above on the Integrated Wholeness Scale. Are you there yet?

Your new codes empower you to cultivate your own noble purpose in life. The soul chooses to love your True Self and others unconditionally, especially through adversity, as you integrate enlightenment and wholeness through forgiveness and new levels of awareness. This is the fuel of miracles.

3) When was the last time you looked into a mirror and saw who you really are without the judgments of the ego mind?

Love is your true nature. Choose to be the love that you are, or by default you choose to listen to the ego mind and stay in fear of never being good enough, beautiful enough, or smart enough. Stay low and lonely on the Integrated Wholeness Scale, or use the miracle that is love to reconnect to the perfection that you are and rise to love or above. This is where you belong. Ignite the secret to your success.

"There is no mistaking love.

You feel it in your heart.

It is the common fibre of life,

the flame that heats our soul,

energizes our spirit and supplies

passion to our lives.

It is our connection to God

and to each other."

–Elizabeth Kubler-Ross,
The Wheel Of Life

THE ULTIMATE MIND SHIFT: AN INTRODUCTION TO QUANTUM NEUTRALITY—THE FIRST STEPS

It is time to ignite the secret to your success.

Restore strength and energy to body, mind, and soul. The Quantum Neutrality Process is the art and science of identifying and neutralizing your blocks and deleting their effects. As you make the ultimate mind shift you heighten your awareness, access your personal power, and make better decisions about life, love, and your relationships.

1. Your information center is your midline, core, spine, and your central and peripheral nervous systems. The components of your information center can be corrected to be strong by closing your eyes and imagining more of your True Self in the form of white light pouring in through the top of your head and filling your whole being. If you are not seeing or feeling the light, don't quit! Keep going until you do; simply use your imagination. Remember a time you sat with the sun pouring through you or felt the heat of a spotlight on your head. If you are still not connecting to the white light, take yourself into the sunshine or sit under a hot spotlight. That's it. You can do this!

As you imagine your True Self in the form of white light filling your being, this corrects the information center, relaxes you and informs the ego mind it is time to sit and stay; to listen and learn without comment.

2. Discover the issue responsible for taking you out of balance by tapping into your intuition. Intuition is a core element of higher awareness. It is the powerhouse within your mainframe. It identifies passwords and deciphers faulty codes running in your human computer. Your intuition is used to access information from the Divine Mind field and helps you determine where you are weak or strong. What is the answer? Concentrate. Focus. Determine to access your intuition and have it work for you.

How many times have you experienced this? Say you're doing a Google search and after only one word, or even just a part of a word, the computer appears to read your mind and in a flash complete thoughts appear. Intuition works in a similar way. The Divine Mind assembles millions of life experiences and provides you with an immediate "Executive Summary."

Intuition is always ready for your use. Some people call it a gut feeling or inner knowing. The more you use it, the stronger it gets and the more effective your corrections become. Your intuition can identify what programs make you feel weak or strong, but if you do not trust it yet, use muscle testing or kinesiology to confirm the source of the weakness.

When you feel discomfort such as fear, negativity or pain a program has been triggered and you need to get neutral. You might think you know what needs to be worked on, but in every case it is never what you think it is. All disease, distress and discomfort first originates within the mind field and only then is it felt as pain. All symptoms begin with a lack of love.

The cause is always found in an ego mind program which shows up as a belief or idea. You brought programs into your life with you as well as acquiring them from your environment. Usually you will not identify or even relate with the original programs as they have been buried deep in the storage section—the unconscious mind—of your computer for so long you have forgotten they were even there.

3. Applying the Quantum Neutrality Process, focus on your information center and say, either aloud or to yourself, "I neutralize all beliefs, ideas, and patterns associated with this program on a physical, mental, emotional, psychological, psychic, or spiritual level." Your intention will determine your results. Don't just say it. Feel it. Mean it.

4. Now say aloud or to yourself, "I delete all karma and habitual thinking related to this program." Feel it and visualize it leaving your body. Feel the weight lifting off your shoulders.

5. With unconditional love, forgive everyone and everything that has hurt you associated with the program you have just corrected, including yourself. Even if you have to start with just one person and a small or trivial issue, forgive everyone and everything involved.

As you follow these steps, the emotional charge around the information in the program dissolves. In fact, you will not be able to find the old emotional feelings and reactions once they have been corrected. Often you will feel a shift in your body once the relevant mental and emotional energy has been discharged in this way.

A feeling of relief is the first sign the program has been corrected and you are neutral to the event. You will feel empowered to move forward, free of the blocks to your inner peace. Your body, mind, and soul will now realign with your personal power and you will be more able to regenerate, rejuvenate, strengthen, and renew your entire energy system.

A QUICK OVERVIEW: LOVE

"It is not how much you do, but how much love you put into the doing that matters."

—*Mother Teresa*

Use these key points from the Divine Mind Code to assist the genie that is love to grant your heart's desire for success in every area of your life.

- Love is a state and an energy, not an emotion. As energy, it is the most powerful energy of the cosmos. It is the catalyst of creation and is infinitely powerful.

- At your very core, love is the perfection of who you really are, unimpeded by ego mind programs.

- As an aspect of your True Self, love is inextricably interwoven with peace, forgiveness, enlightenment, and success in every area of your life.

- Without love, it is impossible to live a PLATINUM life because, more than anything, love facilitates transformation.

- The Divine Mind Code is founded on love. It is characterized by authenticity, openness, transparency, acceptance, empathy, and respect. It always supports the development and growth of more love.

- Fear is simply the manifestation of the ego mind's corrupted software programs. In contrast, love is the

This is an introduction to Quantum Neutrality, a groundbreaking process that is invaluable and life-changing. We treat it more fully in *NEUTRALITY: Go Beyond Positive—Your Key to Freedom*, the sixth book in The CODEBREAKER PLATINUM Series. We also address this in still more depth in our programs, trainings, and live events.

manifestation of the Divine Mind in action. Only love is capable of unlocking the doors to a life filled with happiness and limitless joy.

- The key to enlightenment is to lighten up.

- Divine Love is unconditional, all-encompassing, and infinite. It surpasses the understanding of the logical mind and opens the door to the health and well-being of your body and mind as well as your soul.

- You have a purpose, indeed a noble purpose. Focus on how you can better use your gifts to serve humanity and that will supercharge your perfect divine love relationships.

- Love is a choice you make until it is no longer a choice but your undeniable state of being.

- The people you attract into your life serve you in becoming whole by showing you where you are not whole. Every time someone hurts you, it is an opportunity to ask what program has been triggered that needs to be neutralized.

- When you feel negativity, fear, or pain, you are playing a game, i.e., a program has been triggered, and you have given your ego puppy free rein. Whatever has triggered you that takes you out of love has come about because of your ideas, beliefs, and unconscious programs.

- Use the tools to get neutral. Neutralize everything that causes despair as it arises. This is the path back into love, your PLATINUM life, and the peak state of living in the Divine Mind.

- Love wants to take every opportunity to express kindness, compassion, and consideration no matter where you are.

- The greatest gift you can give yourself or your partner or potential partner is your own wholeness—becoming the best version of you.

- Make your partner's wholeness and happiness your highest priority.

- The frequency of love is the frequency of success.

- Spiritual love is the water that quenches your thirst, frees you from the isolation of separation, and magnetizes even more love into your life. This love does not expect anything in return and is whole unto itself—and just think, this is who you are!

- Love no matter what. Forgive when given the chance. Become ever-vigilant to any judgments that drop in, and drop them like hot cakes.

- Nothing outside yourself can satisfy your longing for love like your True Self can.

- The truth is you have always been worthy of love, you have always been beautiful enough, strong enough, smart enough. You can attune yourself to the frequency of love at any time.

- Like a prayer, these statements form an energy that you send out to the cosmos aligning yourself with the Divine Mind Code.

- Connect fully to the love that you are and unleash the immeasurable power of the Divine Mind. The irresistible magnetic influence of love knows no boundaries.

- Change your thoughts. Love is not something you have to get, give, or do.

- Change your life. Love is the awesome, profoundly fundamental and essential energy that is who you are. You are what you have been looking for.

- Change your world. Be the love you want to see in the world, and your world will become a vibrational match to the energy of love.

- Continue to be a mirror for the love that others are, even if they have programs acting as obstacles to that love.

- Express gratitude for everything in your life, especially all the love, even if it is only coming from your dog or cat right now. You can lose everything that is important to you in the material world, but you will never lose the most precious gift of all, Divine Love. This is your limitless source of creativity and inspiration. Your True Self uses the wisdom and power of Divine Love to recenter you back into what is truly important—where you express the joy of your personal power.

- Your CODEBREAKER PLATINUM password empowers you to cultivate your own noble purpose in life: the evolution of your soul to express your True Self. Loving others unconditionally, especially through adversity, as you integrate enlightenment and wholeness through forgiveness and new levels of awareness, truly is the fuel of miracles.

We are inviting you to make the Ultimate Mind Shift—the shift from the head to the heart, from the ego mind code to the Divine Mind Code. As Deepak Chopra said, "The movement of life is from duality to unity." This is a total paradigm shift. It is the true key to inner peace and to living a PLATINUM life of happiness and love, success and joy.

Don't let your ego mind programs steal your peace and diminish your love.

REMEMBER: IT'S OKAY. IT'S NOT REAL. IT'S JUST YOUR STORY.

"Reality is merely an illusion, albeit a very persistent one."

—Albert Einstein

"Until one is committed there is hesitancy, the chance to draw back, always ineffectiveness. Concerning all acts of initiative (and creation), there is one elementary truth, the ignorance of which kills countless ideas and splendid plans:

That the moment one definitely commits oneself, then Providence moves too. All sorts of things occur to help one that would otherwise never have occurred. A whole stream of events issues from the decision, raising in one's favor all manner of unforeseen incidents and meetings and material assistance, which no man could have dreamt would have come his way.

I have learned a deep respect for one of Goethe's couplets:

Whatever you can do, or dream you can — begin it. Boldness has genius, power, and magic in it."

–W. N. Murray
The Scottish Himalayan Expedition, 1951

You are now ready to move on to the next keyword in the Master Password. As you move forward on life's greatest adventure, and you build upon PEACE and LOVE as your foundation, it is time to take the next step in connecting with the best version of you. Discover how life really works with *AWARENESS*.

AWARENESS: With Awareness, you intuitively see beyond ego mind stories and understand the big picture.

AWARENESS: Discover How Life Really Works is the third book in *The CODEBREAKER PLATINUM Series*. As you use awareness to strengthen your connection with your True Self and the energy frequency of enlightenment, you will super charge your intuition which further empowers your success.

Access the tools and resources at www.TheBiskinds.com.

Collect all eight books in *The CODEBREAKER PLATINUM Series* starting with *PEACE* and *LOVE*.

PEACE: Power Up Your Life
thebiskinds.com/peace

LOVE: Ignite The Secret To Your Success
thebiskinds.com/love

With warmest love and blessings,
Sandra and Daniel

ABOUT SANDRA AND DANIEL

The Biskinds share their expertise in personal transformation as thought leaders, authors, teachers, professional speakers, and consultants. They are also coaches and mentors. Both have had highly successful careers as business entrepreneurs with multi-award winning businesses in the United States of America, Australia, and New Zealand.

Now based in the USA and focused exclusively on personal transformation, Sandra and Daniel are the originators of a groundbreaking body of work introduced in *The CODE-BREAKER PLATINUM Series.* Presented with passion, intensity, grace, and wisdom, the Series is designed to empower individuals to build their own life of happiness, success, and fun — putting passion back into relationships, fulfillment and joy back into work, and restoring and enhancing health, vitality and well-being.

Born in Australia, Sandra has always been an intuitive who spoke to Divine beings from the age of three when she told her mother she was here to work for God. Even through thirty-six death defying surgeries, financial ruin and divorce Sandra's determination to succeed and to find the answers to the eternal questions of life, death, and love led her to become a self-made millionaire by the age of 29. She has diligently worked with some of the greatest spiritual teachers and success coaches throughout the world and is now a highly sought after keynote speaker and workshop leader in personal transformation and enlightenment.

Born in America, Daniel's dream has always been to set people free. To do that, he realized he first had to set himself free. Daniel had a 25-year career as owner/CEO in large scale property development with high profile roles in civic, charitable and industry leadership positions. His training encompassed a wide variety of spiritual traditions and deep experience in the human potential movement as well as advanced business and management education.

When he met an Australian woman at one of her seminars in New Zealand, Daniel knew Sandra would rearrange his life forever. He proposed to her on their first date and they agreed they were married the next time they met. Sixteen years later, they still consider themselves newlyweds.

In their first project together they created a private retreat in New Zealand to host spiritual intensives which, in its first year following completion, won Conde Nast Traveller's highest rating in its Gold List of the world's Top 100 Hotels. It went on to be crowned The World's Best Luxury Coastal Hotel by the World Luxury Hotel Awards in 2010. In 2012 Eagles Nest received the World Travel Awards title of The World's Best Luxury Villa Boutique Resort.

Sandra and Daniel work with highly successful people who are committed to get to the next level in their business and private lives—to be the best versions of themselves. They free their clients to successfully lean in to their lives—completely neutral, fully aware, mindful, and present. As Jack Canfield said, "They have an amazing ability to shift energy and remove blocks on very deep levels."

"Only a life lived for others is a life worthwhile."

—*Albert Einstein*

FROM SANDRA AND DANIEL

Your thoughts are always the key variable in every situation. Training your mind to think thoughts that serve you is your highest priority. And becoming the best version of you is the most rewarding undertaking of all. It is an open-ended process in which we are continually reminded that the means and the ends must always be in harmony and integrity.

We have dedicated our lives to sharing our journey into enlightenment and wholeness. We invite you to share yours with us and move into higher and higher states of Integrated Wholeness together—to truly become the best versions of ourselves.

On our journey we have invested many decades in study, research and development. We have traveled the planet to sit with many leading spiritual teachers and energy masters and in the process have developed a turbo-charged process for rapid change which results in major shifts within minutes as we neutralize blocks. We constantly witness people set free from the debilitating residue of trauma that years of therapy and counseling have been unable to shift. Using the higher awareness produced by The Ultimate Mind Shift Process™, we tap into what scientists call the human mind field to identify the underlying causes of any issue and then use precise frequencies to neutralize them and delete their effects.

Like most people, we have had massive challenges throughout our lives. Using the work we teach we not only survived but thrived. For more than 30 years we have successfully worked with thousands of people around the world and been gratified to achieve amazing results. We invite you to use us and these books as loving guides, mentors and coaches to support you on your journey.

You now have unprecedented opportunity and resources to make a quantum leap in your experience of life and in the evolution of your soul. The decision is in your hands. Empower yourself to transform your life and to change your state to feel better, faster than you believe possible. Regardless of what you have or have not said or done, forgive yourself. Love yourself as we love you—fully, completely, and unconditionally. Embrace your calling and master the exhilarating role of being your own best friend and coach, your own guru.

If you would like to know more about Sandra and Daniel please visit TheBiskinds.com.

APPRECIATION

Throughout our lives we have been blessed to have an enormous number of people make profound contributions to who we have become—and are still becoming. *LOVE: Ignite the Secret To Your Success* is the second of eight books in The CODEBREAKER PLATINUM Series. These books are a distillation of over 30 years of spiritual practice and study, powerful personal transformational experience, and our ongoing journey into becoming the best versions of ourselves.

With incredible gratitude to all the business and success mentors, coaches, transformational teachers and spiritual and mystical masters who have touched our lives with your books, your work shops and more importantly your presence, we say a truly heartfelt thank you. Thank you for your dedication in being the change we all seek and for sharing who you are with the world.

A special thank you to Jack Canfield for taking the time to read *CODEBREAKER* and give us your feedback on a very rough first draft. You told us a book is not ready for publication until it has been rewritten at least six times and encouraged us to get feedback from a minimum of ten beta readers. Well, thanks to you, *CODEBREAKER: Discover The Password To Unlock The Best Version of You* was sent out to over 30 people whose feedback was instrumental in helping us rewrite it more than six times. Each chapter was written as a book in its own right and feedback confirmed the importance of releasing them in the order they appear in the Master Password.

To everyone who has already read and re-read The CODE-BREAKER PLATINUM Series we cannot thank you enough for your support, wisdom and thoughtfulness in making these books better in every way. To all the beta readers, and our editors and developmental editors who shared their ideas on how to simplify and make a deep subject easier to comprehend we are eternally grateful.

Writing these books has been a roller coaster ride of excitement and overwhelming appreciation for so many people. Infinite gratitude goes to Bill Bryant and Sandy Beamer who have devoted months to helping us in the rewriting process. Daily they asked us to give better explanations of concepts that were new to them or they thought needed clarification or simplification. They wanted more examples and more stories to make the teaching more memorable. Their lives have changed because of their total immersion into the information in each book. Can you imagine what a Godsend they were to us? After 30-plus years of committed spiritual transformation practice and study with the one transcendent desire to live an enlightened life, they helped us break down deep concepts that were natural and normal to us into bite size chunks to make it easier to digest and to use in your everyday life.

Deepest thanks and endless love to all our students and coaching and consulting clients whose dedication and courage to move beyond limiting blocks keeps us motivated to find better, faster and more effective processes. You inspire us with your dedication and honor us with your trust.

Our heartfelt thanks goes to our editor, Chris O'Byrne, and his team and to the amazing Mary Guiseffi and Heidi Gress. Mary and Heidi interpreted our cover ideas perfectly and produced ILLUMINATION—our book cover designs.

Finally, we want to thank all our family, and our friends who have become family, for your continued support and love - without love the world would be a cold and unfriendly place instead of the warm, uplifting and inspiring place we are so grateful to experience.

BECOME THE BEST VERSION OF YOU

Empowered Enlightened Inspired

THANK YOU! We hope you enjoyed the second book in The CODEBREAKER PLATINUM Series and you are equipped with more tools to help you achieve freedom from emotional stress and pain and to have the love relationship of your dreams!

You can rate this book, Tweet, and talk about it on Facebook. Please take a moment to do that. We'd be grateful and it will help others who want to have a happier, more meaningful and fulfilled life.

We would also appreciate it if you could leave a short review of the book on Amazon via the link below. It will help us improve this and future books and help others like yourself decide if the books in this series are right for them.

Go here to go to leave a review on Amazon: amzn.to/1Ct9OX0
Check out *PEACE: Power Up Your Life* - TheBiskinds.com/peace
Post to Facebook: facebook.com/TheBiskinds
Tweet about this book: twitter.com/CodebreakerBook

PEACE

*Fully connected to the light of my True Self,
Peace is my natural state.*

PLATINUM

LOVE

*Unconditional love is my essence.
My purpose is to grow, evolve and have fun
expressing the love that I am.*

PLATINUM

AWARENESS

With awareness I intuitively see beyond ego mind stories and understand the big picture.

PLATINUM

TRUST

I trust my True Self can discern the truth in any situation which frees me from fear.

PLATINUM

INTEGRITY

My Integrity never compromises the means for an end so I am always whole and trustworthy.

PLATINUM

NEUTRALITY

Being neutral empowers me to realize freedom and wholeness and to have the life of my dreams.

PLATINUM

UNITY

Integrating unity and oneness makes it natural for me to love and forgive everyone and everything.

PLATINUM

MINDFULNESS

Mindfulness alerts me whenever I need to correct negative thoughts, feelings, and emotions to get neutral to be happy.

PLATINUM